## TABLE OF CONTENTS


Workbook Answers ..... 4
Chapter 1 - Place Value and Number Sense ..... 4
Chapter 2 - Addition ..... 10
Chapter 3 - Subtraction ..... 14
Chapter 4 - Decimals ..... 17
Chapter 5 - Multiplication ..... 21
Chapter 6 - Division ..... 24
Chapter 7 - Geometry ..... 27
Chapter 8 - Measurements ..... 30
Chapter 8 - Fractions ..... 33
Practice Test Answers ..... 37
Practice Test #1 ..... 37
Answers and Explanations ..... 37
Practice Test #2 ..... 42
Answers and Explanations ..... 42
Online Resources ..... 47

# *Workbook Answers*

## *Chapter 1 - Place Value and Number Sense*

**Pg 6**

1.

| Hundred Thousands | Ten Thousands | Thousands | Hundreds | Tens | Ones |
|---|---|---|---|---|---|
| 4 | 2 | 2 | 7 | 1 | 9 |

2.

| Hundred Thousands | Ten Thousands | Thousands | Hundreds | Tens | Ones |
|---|---|---|---|---|---|
| 9 | 8 | 2 | 1 | 2 | 4 |

3.

| Hundred Thousands | Ten Thousands | Thousands | Hundreds | Tens | Ones |
|---|---|---|---|---|---|
| 2 | 6 | 3 | 9 | 2 | 7 |

4.

| Hundred Thousands | Ten Thousands | Thousands | Hundreds | Tens | Ones |
|---|---|---|---|---|---|
| 6 | 2 | 7 | 1 | 4 | 1 |

5.

| Hundred Thousands | Ten Thousands | Thousands | Hundreds | Tens | Ones |
|---|---|---|---|---|---|
| 8 | 9 | 1 | 3 | 6 | 2 |

**Pg 7**

| | | | | | | | |
|---|---|---|---|---|---|---|---|
| 1. | 6 Millions | 1 Hundred Thousands | 3 Ten Thousands | 8 Thousands | 4 Hundreds | 6 Tens | 2 Ones |
| 2. | 3 Millions | 1 Hundred Thousands | 9 Ten Thousands | 4 Thousands | 6 Hundreds | 7 Tens | 5 Ones |
| 3. | 8 Millions | 4 Hundred Thousands | 1 Ten Thousands | 7 Thousands | 2 Hundreds | 0 Tens | 5 Ones |
| 4. | 2 Millions | 7 Hundred Thousands | 6 Ten Thousands | 5 Thousands | 4 Hundreds | 4 Tens | 7 Ones |
| 5. | 5 Millions | 9 Hundred Thousands | 2 Ten Thousands | 5 Thousands | 0 Hundreds | 5 Tens | 7 Ones |

**Pg 8**

1. a. 3
   b. 4
   c. 1,000's
   d. 10's

2. a. 3
   b. 2
   c. 10,000's
   d. 1's

3. a. 7
   b. 4
   c. 10's
   d. 10,000's

4. a. 9
   b. 1
   c. 1's
   d. 1,000's

5. a. 9
   b. 5
   c. 1,000's
   d. 10,000's

| Pg 9 | | Pg 10 | | Pg 11 | |
|---|---|---|---|---|---|
| **No.** | **Answer** | **No.** | **Answer** | **No.** | **Answer** |
| 1 | 900 | 1 | 3,000 | 1 | 80 + 2 |
| 2 | 200 | 2 | 9,000 | 2 | 20 + 9 |
| 3 | 600 | 3 | 1,000 | 3 | 50 + 6 |
| 4 | 600 | 4 | 8,000 | 4 | 70 + 4 |
| 5 | 800 | 5 | 3,000 | 5 | 30 + 5 |
| 6 | 300 | 6 | 4,000 | 6 | 90 + 9 |
| 7 | 200 | 7 | 6,000 | 7 | 200 + 50 |
| 8 | 600 | 8 | 8,000 | 8 | 600 + 20 + 9 |
| 9 | 400 | 9 | 6,000 | 9 | 100 + 50 |
| 10 | 100 | 10 | 2,000 | 10 | 800 + 90 + 2 |
| 11 | 9,000 | 11 | 40,000 | 11 | 900 + 5 |
| 12 | 4,000 | 12 | 20,000 | 12 | 400 + 20 + 7 |
| 13 | 3,000 | 13 | 90,000 | 13 | 20 + 9 |
| 14 | 6,000 | 14 | 60,000 | 14 | 70 + 1 |
| 15 | 7,000 | 15 | 70,000 | 15 | 80 + 6 |
| 16 | 2,000 | 16 | 80,000 | 16 | 50 + 4 |
| 17 | 9,000 | 17 | 30,000 | 17 | 10 + 6 |
| 18 | 6,000 | 18 | 40,000 | 18 | 30 + 8 |
| 19 | 2,000 | 19 | 20,000 | | |
| 20 | 5,000 | 20 | 50,000 | | |
| 21 | 50,000 | 21 | 300,000 | | |
| 22 | 70,000 | 22 | 600,000 | | |
| 23 | 10,000 | 23 | 200,000 | | |
| 24 | 50,000 | 24 | 500,000 | | |
| 25 | 90,000 | 25 | 200,000 | | |
| 26 | 40,000 | 26 | 300,000 | | |
| 27 | 20,000 | 27 | 900,000 | | |
| 28 | 10,000 | 28 | 600,000 | | |
| | | 29 | 800,000 | | |
| | | 30 | 100,000 | | |

| Pg 12 | | Pg 13 | |
|---|---|---|---|
| No. | Answer | No. | Answer |
| 1 | 100 + 50 + 6 | 1 | 9,281 / 9,289 / 92,891 / 96,381 |
| 2 | 600 + 50 + 8 | 2 | 2,313 / 22,311 / 23,111 / 23,112 |
| 3 | 200 + 90 + 5 | 3 | 7,855 / 7,856 / 78,855 / 78,856 |
| 4 | 400 + 30 + 1 | 4 | 1,111 / 10,112 / 11,112 / 11,131 |
| 5 | 500 + 60 + 7 | 5 | 4,316 / 4,326 / 44,326 / 44,436 |
| 6 | 100 + 50 + 5 | 6 | 3,289 / 3,818 / 3,819 / 3,891 |
| 7 | 800 + 30 + 2 | 7 | 57,211 / 57,289 / 57,500 / 57,891 |
| 8 | 300 + 90 + 4 | 8 | 6,255 / 6,552 / 60,255 / 66,252 |
| 9 | 2,000 + 500 + 90 + 1 | 9 | 15,247 / 15,248 / 15,249 / 15,250 |
| 10 | 8,000 + 900 + 40 + 2 | 10 | 9,546 / 9,564 / 92,564 / 93,564 |
| 11 | 4,000 + 100 + 50 +4 | 11 | 8,219 / 84,218 / 84,219 / 84,921 |
| 12 | 6,000 + 300 + 80 + 7 | | |
| 13 | 1,000 + 500 + 80 + 2 | | |
| 14 | 3,000 + 500 + 70 + 8 | | |
| 15 | 40,000 + 4,000 + 600 + 50 + 8 | | |
| 16 | 70,000 + 3,000 + 400 + 30 + 5 | | |
| 17 | 90,000 + 5,000 + 200 + 60 + 1 | | |
| 18 | 30,000 + 7,000 + 800 + 70 + 2 | | |
| | | | |

| Pg 14 | |
|---|---|
| No. | Answer |
| 1 | 100,280 / 100,289 / 100,381 / 100,891 |
| 2 | 51,110 / 512,101 / 512,112 / 512,123 |
| 3 | 855,622 / 856,628 / 856,629 / 865,622 |
| 4 | 633,601 / 634,101 / 634,209 / 635,700 |
| 5 | 20,115 / 21,115 / 231,115 / 231,150 |
| 6 | 546,020 / 546,029 / 546,030 / 546,209 |
| 7 | 355,111 / 355,891 / 375,375 / 375,787 |
| 8 | 23,151 / 237,151 / 239,151 / 240,151 |
| 9 | 145,280 / 145,381 / 146,891 / 155,289 |
| 10 | 20,722 / 266,722 / 269,722 / 269,772 |
| 11 | 90,280 / 90,281 / 90,821 / 990,281 |
| 12 | 7,537 / 75,337 / 76,337 / 175,337 |

| Pg 15 | | Pg 16 | |
|---|---|---|---|
| **No.** | **Answer** | **No.** | **Answer** |
| 1 | 10,495 \| 11,005 | 1 | 980,311 \| 980,411 |
| 2 | 98,311 \| 98,411 | 2 | 622,001 \| 620,001 |
| 3 | 61,001 \| 63,001 | 3 | 282,929 \| 283,029 |
| 4 | 22,929 \| 23,029 | 4 | 694,647 \| 694,667 |
| 5 | 81,657 \| 83,657 | 5 | 113,729 \| 114,729 |
| 6 | 2,495 \| 2,505 | 6 | 349,001 \| 351,001 |
| 7 | 12,303 \| 13,303 | 7 | 524,303 \| 525,303 |
| 8 | 41,370 \| 43,370 | 8 | 810,370 \| 820,370 |
| 9 | 72,126 \| 72,133 | 9 | 156,119 \| 456,119 |
| 10 | 34,776 \| 35,776 | 10 | 619,776 \| 629,776 |
| 11 | 69,061 \| 89,061 | 11 | 120,383 \| 125,383 |
| | | 12 | 350,303 \| 360,303 |

# Chapter 2 – Addition

| Pg 18 | | Pg 19 | | Pg 20 | |
|---|---|---|---|---|---|
| **No.** | **Answer** | **No.** | **Answer** | **No.** | **Answer** |
| 1 | 81 | 1 | 92 | 1 | 73 |
| 2 | 65 | 2 | 103 | 2 | 163 |
| 3 | 167 | 3 | 178 | 3 | 135 |
| 4 | 51 | 4 | 109 | 4 | 182 |
| 5 | 124 | 5 | 78 | 5 | 98 |
| 6 | 49 | 6 | 145 | 6 | 247 |
| 7 | 46 | 7 | 61 | 7 | 141 |
| 8 | 38 | 8 | 94 | 8 | 130 |
| 9 | 163 | 9 | 119 | 9 | 157 |
| 10 | 65 | 10 | 22 | 10 | 76 |
| 11 | 90 | 11 | 103 | 11 | 178 |
| 12 | 117 | 12 | 107 | 12 | 87 |
| 13 | 72 | 13 | 72 | 13 | 57 |
| 14 | 21 | 14 | 91 | 14 | 106 |
| 15 | 113 | 15 | 92 | 15 | 161 |
| | | 16 | 155 | 16 | 146 |
| | | 17 | 136 | 17 | 236 |
| | | 18 | 125 | 18 | 138 |
| | | 19 | 140 | 19 | 117 |
| | | 20 | 162 | 20 | 286 |

| Pg 21 | | Pg 22 | | Pg 23 | |
|---|---|---|---|---|---|
| **No.** | **Answer** | **No.** | **Answer** | **No.** | **Answer** |
| 1 | 114 | 1 | 64 apples | 1 | 819 |
| 2 | 171 | 2 | 56 minutes | 2 | 1,309 |
| 3 | 99 | 3 | 92 points | 3 | 156 |
| 4 | 120 | 4 | 173 minutes | 4 | 756 |
| 5 | 184 | | | 5 | 456 |
| 6 | 168 | | | 6 | 253 |
| 7 | 135 | | | 7 | 837 |
| 8 | 97 | | | 8 | 1,221 |
| 9 | 211 | | | 9 | 707 |
| 10 | 156 | | | 10 | 980 |
| 11 | 216 | | | | |
| 12 | 146 | | | | |
| 13 | 80 | | | | |
| 14 | 197 | | | | |
| 15 | 193 | | | | |
| 16 | 181 | | | | |
| 17 | 98 | | | | |
| 18 | 134 | | | | |
| 19 | 207 | | | | |
| 20 | 49 | | | | |

| Pg 24 | | Pg 25 | | Pg 26 | |
|---|---|---|---|---|---|
| **No.** | **Answer** | **No.** | **Answer** | **No.** | **Answer** |
| 1 | 610 | 1 | 839 | 1 | 1,168 |
| 2 | 444 | 2 | 634 | 2 | 1,034 |
| 3 | 1,057 | 3 | 1,146 | 3 | 921 |
| 4 | 718 | 4 | 1,292 | 4 | 1,136 |
| 5 | 1,074 | 5 | 1,294 | 5 | 1,741 |
| 6 | 1,062 | 6 | 1,488 | 6 | 835 |
| 7 | 1,023 | 7 | 1,877 | 7 | 1,115 |
| 8 | 1,600 | 8 | 1,201 | 8 | 592 |
| 9 | 511 | 9 | 1,644 | 9 | 1,784 |
| 10 | 853 | 10 | 1,154 | 10 | 1,408 |
| 11 | 965 | 11 | 1,038 | 11 | 1,788 |
| 12 | 767 | 12 | 1,305 | 12 | 1,737 |
| 13 | 611 | 13 | 1,812 | 13 | 1,609 |
| 14 | 365 | 14 | 1,130 | 14 | 630 |
| 15 | 881 | 15 | 1,404 | 15 | 1,948 |
| 16 | 1,714 | 16 | 1,961 | 16 | 1,619 |
| 17 | 857 | 17 | 1,668 | 17 | 1,040 |
| 18 | 1,648 | 18 | 1,817 | 18 | 1,513 |
| 19 | 1,578 | 19 | 1,712 | 19 | 1,416 |
| 20 | 640 | 20 | 1,174 | 20 | 1,086 |

| Pg 27 | | Pg 28 | | Pg 29 | | Pg 30 | |
|---|---|---|---|---|---|---|---|
| **No.** | **Answer** | **No.** | **Answer** | **No.** | **Answer** | **No.** | **Answer** |
| 1 | 12,301 | 1 | 6,515 | 1 | 51,648 | 1 | 104,349 |
| 2 | 10,761 | 2 | 16,834 | 2 | 100,997 | 2 | 49,815 |
| 3 | 17,388 | 3 | 12,670 | 3 | 100,116 | 3 | 70,804 |
| 4 | 5,201 | 4 | 13,229 | 4 | 40099 | 4 | 107,345 |
| 5 | 18,354 | 5 | 16,342 | 5 | 53,040 | 5 | 119,008 |
| 6 | 3,656 | 6 | 8,877 | 6 | 144,064 | 6 | 106,269 |
| 7 | 5,827 | 7 | 6300 | 7 | 101,610 | 7 | 133,061 |
| 8 | 8,464 | 8 | 11,866 | 8 | 62,008 | 8 | 40,277 |
| 9 | 11,656 | 9 | 13,940 | 9 | 73,875 | 9 | 72,695 |
| 10 | 3,875 | 10 | 16,715 | 10 | 71,664 | 10 | 34,262 |
| 11 | 8,347 | 11 | 15,009 | 11 | 47,770 | 11 | 72,436 |
| 12 | 7,886 | 12 | 6,461 | 12 | 37,380 | 12 | 99,053 |
| 13 | 14,419 | 13 | 15,177 | 13 | 105,374 | 13 | 137,107 |
| 14 | 5,328 | 14 | 15,408 | 14 | 181,336 | 14 | 82,013 |
| 15 | 10,061 | 15 | 13,512 | 15 | 63,471 | 15 | 69,809 |
| 16 | 9,571 | 16 | 24,745 | 16 | 115,422 | 16 | 143,052 |
| 17 | 5,567 | 17 | 10,693 | 17 | 116,456 | 17 | 81,492 |
| 18 | 7,669 | 18 | 14,319 | 18 | 58,785 | 18 | 88,374 |
| 19 | 6,145 | 19 | 14,792 | 19 | 88,523 | 19 | 106,406 |
| 20 | 4,859 | 20 | 14,112 | 20 | 123,973 | 20 | 111,110 |

# Chapter 3 – Subtraction

| Pg 32 | | Pg 33 | | Pg 34 | | Pg 35 | |
|---|---|---|---|---|---|---|---|
| **No.** | **Answer** | **No.** | **Answer** | **No.** | **Answer** | **No.** | **Answer** |
| 1 | 29 | 1 | 9 | 1 | 9 | 1 | 32 |
| 2 | 26 | 2 | 59 | 2 | 8 | 2 | 44 |
| 3 | 79 | 3 | 18 | 3 | 9 | 3 | 64 |
| 4 | 27 | 4 | 59 | 4 | 2 | 4 | 24 |
| 5 | 47 | 5 | 38 | 5 | 1 | | |
| 6 | 36 | 6 | 23 | 6 | 3 | | |
| 7 | 23 | 7 | 52 | 7 | 4 | | |
| 8 | 9 | 8 | 9 | 8 | 9 | | |
| 9 | 68 | 9 | 19 | 9 | 2 | | |
| 10 | 24 | 10 | 3 | 10 | 7 | | |
| 11 | 28 | 11 | 27 | 11 | 2 | | |
| 12 | 28 | 12 | 14 | 12 | 1 | | |
| 13 | 37 | 13 | 15 | 13 | 3 | | |
| 14 | 19 | 14 | 21 | 14 | 3 | | |
| 15 | 47 | 15 | 25 | 15 | 1 | | |
| | | 16 | 14 | 16 | 2 | | |
| | | 17 | 41 | 17 | 6 | | |
| | | 18 | 19 | 18 | 1 | | |
| | | 19 | 35 | 19 | 5 | | |
| | | 20 | 29 | 20 | 2 | | |

| Pg 36 | | Pg 37 | | Pg 38 | | Pg 39 | |
|---|---|---|---|---|---|---|---|
| **No.** | **Answer** | **No.** | **Answer** | **No.** | **Answer** | **No.** | **Answer** |
| 1 | 155 | 1 | 149 | 1 | 2 | 1 | 1,112 |
| 2 | 23 | 2 | 244 | 2 | 2 | 2 | 1,111 |
| 3 | 439 | 3 | 460 | 3 | 8 | 3 | 3,781 |
| 4 | 489 | 4 | 319 | 4 | 4 | 4 | 2,779 |
| 5 | 139 | 5 | 235 | 5 | 2 | 5 | 1,756 |
| 6 | 266 | 6 | 43 | 6 | 1 | 6 | 6,487 |
| 7 | 96 | 7 | 508 | 7 | 5 | 7 | 7,511 |
| 8 | 158 | 8 | 33 | 8 | 5 | 8 | 2,264 |
| 9 | 115 | 9 | 657 | 9 | 8 | 9 | 524 |
| 10 | 179 | 10 | 149 | 10 | 5 | 10 | 5,685 |
| 11 | 828 | 11 | 245 | 11 | 5 | 11 | 327 |
| 12 | 50 | 12 | 142 | 12 | 4 | 12 | 2,047 |
| 13 | 158 | 13 | 295 | 13 | 1 | 13 | 4,635 |
| 14 | 219 | 14 | 413 | 14 | 1 | 14 | 2,059 |
| 15 | 276 | 15 | 116 | 15 | 5 | 15 | 5,475 |
| | | 16 | 159 | 16 | 9 | 16 | 2,889 |
| | | 17 | 113 | 17 | 1 | 17 | 1,454 |
| | | 18 | 283 | 18 | 3 | 18 | 916 |
| | | 19 | 424 | 19 | 1 | 19 | 2,755 |
| | | 20 | 151 | 20 | 1 | 20 | 2,747 |

| Pg 40 | | Pg 41 | | Pg 42 | |
|---|---|---|---|---|---|
| No. | Answer | No. | Answer | No. | Answer |
| 1 | 1,616 | 1 | 13,148 | 1 | 1,697 |
| 2 | 1,158 | 2 | 15,814 | 2 | 40,444 |
| 3 | 488 | 3 | 22,552 | 3 | 13,887 |
| 4 | 1,634 | 4 | 4,247 | 4 | 22,986 |
| 5 | 1,159 | 5 | 56,697 | 5 | 15,585 |
| 6 | 2,858 | 6 | 28,313 | 6 | 25,802 |
| 7 | 2,215 | 7 | 34,340 | 7 | 32,578 |
| 8 | 6,651 | 8 | 36,202 | 8 | 36,857 |
| 9 | 3,491 | 9 | 20,488 | 9 | 17,909 |
| 10 | 888 | 10 | 24,740 | 10 | 15,799 |
| 11 | 2,464 | 11 | 13,056 | 11 | 21,239 |
| 12 | 4,405 | 12 | 4,166 | 12 | 31,847 |
| 13 | 1,109 | 13 | 38,183 | 13 | 42,887 |
| 14 | 4,465 | 14 | 36,482 | 14 | 1,193 |
| 15 | 3,117 | 15 | 22,675 | 15 | 36,487 |
| 16 | 3,280 | 16 | 19,121 | 16 | 52,142 |
| 17 | 4,384 | 17 | 18,498 | 17 | 18,489 |
| 18 | 3,409 | 18 | 26,282 | 18 | 21,529 |
| 19 | 2,135 | 19 | 1,348 | 19 | 17,435 |
| 20 | 6,933 | 20 | 37,376 | 20 | 44,217 |

# Chapter 4 - Decimals

| Pg 44 | | Pg 45 | | Pg 46 | |
|---|---|---|---|---|---|
| **No.** | **Answer** | **No.** | **Answer** | **No.** | **Answer** |
| 1 | 3.59 | 1 | 15.95 | 1 | $5.03 |
| 2 | 7.83 | 2 | 664.48 | 2 | $11.63 |
| 3 | 16.11 | 3 | 27.49 | 3 | $9.22 |
| 4 | 14.16 | 4 | 40.97 | 4 | $6.40 |
| 5 | 10.43 | 5 | 1,374.41 | 5 | $12.75 |
| 6 | 74.36 | 6 | 622.28 | 6 | $22.27 |
| | | 7 | 10.53 | 7 | $22.53 |
| | | 8 | 54.25 | 8 | $19.64 |
| | | 9 | 118 | 9 | $11.93 |
| | | | | 10 | $12.47 |
| | | | | 11 | $15.96 |
| | | | | 12 | $14.76 |
| | | | | 13 | $22.28 |
| | | | | 14 | $20.55 |
| | | | | 15 | $35.21 |
| | | | | 16 | $20.28 |

| Pg 47 | | Pg 48 | | Pg 49 | | Pg 50 | |
|---|---|---|---|---|---|---|---|
| **No.** | **Answer** | **No.** | **Answer** | **No.** | **Answer** | **No.** | **Answer** |
| 1 | $13.45 | 1 | $10.16 | 1 | 52.64 | 1 | 93 |
| 2 | $10.48 | 2 | $6.23 | 2 | 7.2 | 2 | 13 |
| 3 | $10.46 | 3 | $17.64 | 3 | 38.28 | 3 | 33 |
| 4 | $6.90 | 4 | $13.64 | 4 | 15 | 4 | 25 |
| 5 | $139.25 | 5 | $17.50 | | | 5 | 58 |
| 6 | $82.89 | 6 | $96.27 | | | 6 | 65 |
| 7 | $42.52 | 7 | $107.95 | | | 7 | 83 |
| 8 | $122.37 | 8 | $101.99 | | | 8 | 42 |
| 9 | $161.05 | 9 | $40.12 | | | 9 | 69 |
| 10 | $93.44 | 10 | $75.61 | | | 10 | 20 |
| 11 | $92.59 | 11 | $170.83 | | | 11 | 34 |
| 12 | $110.41 | 12 | $161.41 | | | 12 | 32 |
| 13 | $163.19 | 13 | $354.25 | | | 13 | 77 |
| 14 | $630.62 | 14 | $1,184.55 | | | 14 | 72 |
| 15 | $172.16 | 15 | $1,530.84 | | | 15 | 12 |
| 16 | $639.56 | 16 | $533.92 | | | 16 | 44 |
| 17 | $1,145.28 | 17 | $1,460.97 | | | 17 | 46 |
| 18 | $1,404.49 | 18 | $1,101.03 | | | 18 | 56 |
| 19 | $1,420.69 | 19 | $1,870.40 | | | 19 | 21 |
| 20 | $1,330.29 | 20 | $1,003.80 | | | 20 | 19 |

| Pg 51 | | Pg 52 | | Pg 53 | | Pg 54 | |
|---|---|---|---|---|---|---|---|
| **No.** | **Answer** | **No.** | **Answer** | **No.** | **Answer** | **No.** | **Answer** |
| 1 | 893 | 1 | 2.16 | 1 | 4.02 | 1 | $2.47 |
| 2 | 113 | 2 | 34.62 | 2 | 50.35 | 2 | $3.14 |
| 3 | 133 | 3 | 4.65 | 3 | 14.81 | 3 | $3.18 |
| 4 | 25 | 4 | 326.28 | 4 | 42.91 | 4 | $1.86 |
| 5 | 57 | 5 | 854.43 | 5 | 1.73 | 5 | $1.15 |
| 6 | 765 | 6 | 68.99 | 6 | 581.61 | 6 | $1.85 |
| 7 | 22 | | | 7 | 8.43 | 7 | $3.77 |
| 8 | 342 | | | 8 | 255.15 | 8 | $2.30 |
| 9 | 318 | | | 9 | 801.15 | 9 | $3.13 |
| 10 | 920 | | | | | 10 | $3.29 |
| 11 | 94 | | | | | 11 | $0.39 |
| 12 | 32 | | | | | 12 | $3.05 |
| 13 | 57 | | | | | 13 | $4.79 |
| 14 | 672 | | | | | 14 | $22.28 |
| 15 | 813 | | | | | 15 | $13.54 |
| 16 | 544 | | | | | 16 | $10.98 |
| 17 | 35 | | | | | 17 | $7.77 |
| 18 | 812 | | | | | 18 | $14.85 |
| 19 | 122 | | | | | 19 | $7.77 |
| 20 | 698 | | | | | 20 | $9.01 |

| Pg 55 | | Pg 56 | |
|---|---|---|---|
| **No.** | **Answer** | **No.** | **Answer** |
| 1 | $7.84 | 1 | $12.18 |
| 2 | $20.53 | 2 | $3.21 |
| 3 | $14.50 | 3 | $3.18 |
| 4 | $13.06 | 4 | $30.10 |
| 5 | $30.41 | | |
| 6 | $5.02 | | |
| 7 | $12.22 | | |
| 8 | $15.38 | | |
| 9 | $8.38 | | |
| 10 | $18.68 | | |
| 11 | $27.95 | | |
| 12 | $77.98 | | |
| 13 | $31.36 | | |
| 14 | $132.06 | | |
| 15 | $164.32 | | |
| 16 | $930.40 | | |
| 17 | $53.56 | | |
| 18 | $148.72 | | |
| 19 | $390.26 | | |
| 20 | $33.04 | | |

# Chapter 5 – Multiplication

| Pg 60 | | Pg 61 | | Pg 62 | | Pg 63 | |
|---|---|---|---|---|---|---|---|
| **No.** | **Answer** | **No.** | **Answer** | **No.** | **Answer** | **No.** | **Answer** |
| 1 | 48 | 1 | 260 | 1 | 440 | 1 | 820 |
| 2 | 93 | 2 | 710 | 2 | 1780 | 2 | 590 |
| 3 | 86 | 3 | 670 | 3 | 2600 | 3 | 360 |
| 4 | 77 | 4 | 220 | 4 | 1170 | 4 | 910 |
| 5 | 55 | 5 | 380 | 5 | 1440 | 5 | 270 |
| 6 | 88 | 6 | 840 | 6 | 980 | 6 | 600 |
| 7 | 99 | 7 | 190 | 7 | 180 | 7 | 950 |
| 8 | 18 | 8 | 180 | 8 | 2640 | 8 | 890 |
| 9 | 84 | 9 | 940 | 9 | 4600 | 9 | 430 |
| 10 | 66 | 10 | 290 | 10 | 4690 | 10 | 270 |
| | | | | 11 | 670 | 11 | 560 |
| | | | | 12 | 1260 | 12 | 390 |
| | | | | 13 | 270 | 13 | 75 |
| | | | | 14 | 6750 | 14 | 10 |
| | | | | 15 | 1500 | 15 | 88 |
| | | | | 16 | 1320 | 16 | 62 |
| | | | | 17 | 820 | 17 | 59 |
| | | | | 18 | 1650 | 18 | 1 |
| | | | | 19 | 2250 | | |
| | | | | 20 | 5490 | | |

| Pg 64 | | Pg 65 | | Pg 66 | | Pg 67 | |
|---|---|---|---|---|---|---|---|
| **No.** | **Answer** | **No.** | **Answer** | **No.** | **Answer** | **No.** | **Answer** |
| 1 | 92 | 1 | 84 | 1 | 284 | 1 | 1,302 |
| 2 | 406 | 2 | 150 | 2 | 663 | 2 | 663 |
| 3 | 172 | 3 | 52 | 3 | 682 | 3 | 1,705 |
| 4 | 261 | 4 | 558 | 4 | 484 | 4 | 1,732 |
| 5 | 180 | 5 | 198 | 5 | 698 | 5 | 6,282 |
| 6 | 220 | 6 | 425 | 6 | 848 | 6 | 848 |
| 7 | 288 | 7 | 182 | 7 | 396 | 7 | 396 |
| 8 | 495 | 8 | 176 | 8 | 466 | 8 | 1,864 |
| 9 | 198 | 9 | 288 | 9 | 696 | 9 | 2,088 |
| 10 | 354 | 10 | 342 | 10 | 282 | 10 | 1,098 |
| | | 11 | 144 | 11 | 636 | 11 | 4,823 |
| | | 12 | 264 | 12 | 336 | 12 | 2,995 |
| | | 13 | 410 | | | 13 | 7,888 |
| | | 14 | 261 | | | 14 | 738 |
| | | 15 | 264 | | | 15 | 3,908 |
| | | 16 | 236 | | | 16 | 1,110 |
| | | 17 | 234 | | | 17 | 2,740 |
| | | 18 | 378 | | | 18 | 2,432 |
| | | 19 | 475 | | | 19 | 8,640 |
| | | 20 | 276 | | | 20 | 1,590 |

| Pg 68 | | Pg 69 | |
|---|---|---|---|
| No. | Answer | No. | Answer |
| 1 | 735 | 1 | 3,283 |
| 2 | 156 | 2 | 360 |
| 3 | 1,188 | 3 | 1,764 |
| 4 | 3,240 | 4 | 783 |
| 5 | 950 | 5 | 1,716 |
| 6 | 4,620 | 6 | 5,040 |
| 7 | 2,553 | 7 | 2,244 |
| 8 | 667 | 8 | 957 |
| 9 | 4,424 | 9 | 4,851 |
| 10 | 5,544 | 10 | 4,130 |
| | | 11 | 1,053 |
| | | 12 | 408 |
| | | 13 | 3,182 |
| | | 14 | 913 |
| | | 15 | 5,529 |
| | | 16 | 4,950 |
| | | 17 | 1,650 |
| | | 18 | 2,924 |
| | | 19 | 3,404 |
| | | 20 | 494 |

# Chapter 6 – Division

| Pg 72 | | Pg 73 | | Pg 74 | | Pg 75 | |
|---|---|---|---|---|---|---|---|
| **No.** | **Answer** | **No.** | **Answer** | **No.** | **Answer** | **No.** | **Answer** |
| 1 | 3 | 1 | 2 r 2 | 1 | 4 r 1 | 1 | 36 |
| 2 | 8 | 2 | 5 | 2 | 2 r 3 | 2 | 54 |
| 3 | 6 | 3 | 4 r 1 | 3 | 16 r 1 | 3 | 60 |
| 4 | 4 | 4 | 4 r 7 | 4 | 5 | 4 | 100 |
| 5 | 9 | 5 | 10 r 2 | 5 | 5 r 2 | 5 | 6 |
| 6 | 7 | 6 | 9 r 4 | 6 | 4 r 8 | 6 | 49 |
| 7 | 3 | 7 | 12 r 1 | 7 | 6 r 4 | 7 | 10 |
| 8 | 8 | 8 | 14 r 1 | 8 | 4 r 4 | 8 | 45 |
| 9 | 3 | | | 9 | 6 r 4 | 9 | 64 |
| 10 | 3 | | | 10 | 38 r 1 | 10 | 288 |
| 11 | 9 | | | 11 | 12 r 3 | 11 | 63 |
| 12 | 10 | | | 12 | 30 r 1 | 12 | 33 |
| 13 | 4 | | | 13 | 8 r 2 | 13 | 54 |
| 14 | 5 | | | 14 | 12 r 2 | 14 | 24 |
| 15 | 1 | | | 15 | 6 r 1 | | |
| 16 | 11 | | | | | | |
| 17 | 7 | | | | | | |
| 18 | 15 | | | | | | |
| 19 | 3 | | | | | | |
| 20 | 8 | | | | | | |

| Pg 76 | | Pg 77 | | Pg 78 | | Pg 79 | |
|---|---|---|---|---|---|---|---|
| No. | Answer | No. | Answer | No. | Answer | No. | Answer |
| 1 | 8 | 1 | $33 | 1 | 28 r 1 | 1 | 16 r 2 |
| 2 | 11 | 2 | 7 kids | 2 | 24 | 2 | 21 r 2 |
| 3 | 2 | 3 | 3 dolls | 3 | 16 r 1 | 3 | 42 r 1 |
| 4 | 6 | 4 | 9 cars and trucks | 4 | 28 r 1 | 4 | 24 r 3 |
| 5 | 5 | | | 5 | 18 r 1 | 5 | 18 |
| 6 | 12 | | | 6 | 13 r 2 | 6 | 12 r 5 |
| 7 | 4 | | | 7 | 14 r 3 | 7 | 16 r 1 |
| 8 | 9 | | | 8 | 14 | 8 | 29 r 1 |
| 9 | 4 | | | | | 9 | 25 r 1 |
| 10 | 6 | | | | | 10 | 23 |
| 11 | 6 | | | | | 11 | 14 r 5 |
| 12 | 9 | | | | | 12 | 14 r 2 |
| 13 | 8 | | | | | | |
| 14 | 9 | | | | | | |

| Pg 80 | | Pg 81 | | Pg 82 | | Pg 83 | |
|---|---|---|---|---|---|---|---|
| No. | Answer | No. | Answer | No. | Answer | No. | Answer |
| 1 | 246 r 3 | 1 | 164 r 3 | 1 | 11 | 1 | 32 |
| 2 | 49 r 3 | 2 | 171 r 2 | 2 | 22 | 2 | 48 |
| 3 | 296 | 3 | 206 r 3 | 3 | 8 | 3 | 54 |
| 4 | 256 r 1 | 4 | 89 r 3 | 4 | 33 | 4 | 52 |
| 5 | 216 r 3 | 5 | 32 r 1 | 5 | 21 | 5 | 71 |
| 6 | 186 r 4 | 6 | 382 | 6 | 22 | 6 | 60 |
| | | 7 | 51 | | | | |
| | | 8 | 461 r 1 | | | | |
| | | 9 | 144 r 1 | | | | |
| | | 10 | 106 r 2 | | | | |
| | | 11 | 46 r 4 | | | | |
| | | 12 | 81 r 1 | | | | |
| | | 13 | 133 r 6 | | | | |
| | | 14 | 299 r 2 | | | | |
| | | 15 | 130 r 1 | | | | |
| | | | | | | | |

| Pg 84 | |
|---|---|
| **No.** | **Answer** |
| 1 | 84 |
| 2 | 20 |
| 3 | 140 |
| | |

# *Chapter 7 - Geometry*

| Pg 87 | | Pg 89 | | Pg 90 | |
|---|---|---|---|---|---|
| **No.** | **Answer** | **No.** | **Answer** | **No.** | **Answer** |
| 1 | 7, heptagon | 1 | cube | 1 | isosceles |
| 2 | 4, square | 2 | cylinder | 2 | right |
| 3 | 8, octagon | 3 | sphere | 3 | isosceles |
| 4 | 1, circle | 4 | prism | 4 | scalene |
| 5 | 6, hexagon | 5 | pyramid | 5 | equilateral |
| 6 | 4, trapezoid | 6 | cuboid | 6 | scalene |
| 7 | 9, nonagon | 7 | cone | 7 | right |
| 8 | 5, pentagon | 8 | cube | 8 | equilateral |
| 9 | 4, rectangle | 9 | sphere | | |
| 10 | 10, decagon | 10 | prism | | |
| 11 | 6, hexagon | 11 | cuboid | | |
| 12 | 3, triangle | 12 | cone | | |
| 13 | 8, octagon | 13 | cylinder | | |
| 14 | 9, nonagon | 14 | pyramid | | |
| 15 | 4, square | 15 | cube | | |
| 16 | 6, hexagon | 16 | prism | | |

| Pg 91 | | Pg 92 | |
|---|---|---|---|
| **No.** | **Answer** | **No.** | **Answer** |
| 1 | vertex | 1 | perpendicular |
| 2 | ray | 2 | parallel |
| 3 | line segment | 3 | intersecting |
| 4 | point | 4 | parallel |
| 5 | ray | 5 | intersecting |
| 6 | line segment | 6 | perpendicular |
| 7 | vertex | 7 | intersecting |
| 8 | line | 8 | parallel |
| 9 | vertex | 9 | perpendicular |
| 10 | point | 10 | intersecting |
| 11 | line | 11 | parallel |
| 12 | line segment | 12 | perpendicular |

| Pg 93 | | Pg 94 | |
|---|---|---|---|
| **No.** | **Answer** | **No.** | **Answer** |
| 1 | obtuse | 1 | 36 sq. in |
| 2 | right | 2 | 36 sq. ft |
| 3 | acute | 3 | 441 sq. in |
| 4 | obtuse | 4 | 100 sq. ft |
| 5 | right | 5 | 144 sq. yd |
| 6 | obtuse | 6 | 81 sq. in |
| 7 | right | | |
| 8 | acute | | |
| 9 | acute | | |
| 10 | right | | |
| 11 | obtuse | | |
| 12 | acute | | |

| Pg 95 | | Pg 96 | |
|---|---|---|---|
| **No.** | **Answer** | **No.** | **Answer** |
| 1 | 140yd | 1 | 18yd |
| 2 | 25ft | 2 | 39in |
| 3 | 245in | 3 | 38ft |
| 4 | 125ft | 4 | 70yd |
| 5 | 175in | 5 | 290in |
| 6 | 163yd | 6 | 216ft |
| | | 7 | 60ft |
| | | 8 | 75in |
| | | 9 | 48yd |

| Pg 97 | | Pg 98 | | Pg 99 | |
|---|---|---|---|---|---|
| No. | Answer | No. | Answer | No. | Answer |
| 1 | 3 $ft^3$ | 1 | 20 | 1 | 500 $in^3$ |
| 2 | 4 $ft^3$ | 2 | 30 | 2 | 128 $ft^3$ |
| 3 | 6 $ft^3$ | 3 | 24 | 3 | 160 $in^3$ |
| 4 | 5 $ft^3$ | 4 | 36 | 4 | 720 $ft^3$ |
| 5 | 6 $ft^3$ | 5 | 48 | 5 | 240 $in^3$ |
| 6 | 8 $ft^3$ | 6 | 96 | 6 | 400 $ft^3$ |
| 7 | 8 $ft^3$ | 7 | 24 | 7 | 360 $in^3$ |
| 8 | 7 $ft^3$ | 8 | 30 | 8 | 245 $ft^3$ |
| 9 | 7 $ft^3$ | 9 | 60 | 9 | 162 $in^3$ |

# *Chapter 8 - Measurements*

| Pg 102 | | Pg 103 | | Pg 104 | |
|---|---|---|---|---|---|
| **No.** | **Answer** | **No.** | **Answer** | **No.** | **Answer** |
| 1 | 60 pounds | 1 | 3 lb | 1 | inches |
| 2 | 2 tons | 2 | 512 oz | 2 | feet |
| 3 | 5 pounds | 3 | 2 T | 3 | inches |
| 4 | 37 pounds | 4 | 5 lb | 4 | feet |
| | | 5 | 32 oz | 5 | feet |
| | | 6 | 128 oz | 6 | inches |
| | | 7 | 6,000 lb | | |
| | | 8 | 96 oz | | |
| | | 9 | 1 lb | | |
| | | 10 | 6 T | | |

| Pg 105 | | Pg 106 | | Pg 107 | |
|---|---|---|---|---|---|
| **No.** | **Answer** | **No.** | **Answer** | **No.** | **Answer** |
| 1 | > | 1 | 2 1/4 | 1 | 110 |
| 2 | < | 2 | 5 1/2 | 2 | 84 |
| 3 | = | 3 | 4 1/2 | 3 | 117 |
| 4 | > | 4 | 3 3/4 | 4 | 123 |
| 5 | > | 5 | 1 3/4 | 5 | 183 |
| 6 | < | | | | |
| 7 | = | | | | |
| 8 | = | | | | |
| 9 | < | | | | |
| 10 | < | | | | |
| 11 | > | | | | |
| 12 | < | | | | |
| 13 | < | | | | |
| 14 | < | | | | |
| 15 | > | | | | |
| 16 | < | | | | |

## Pg 108

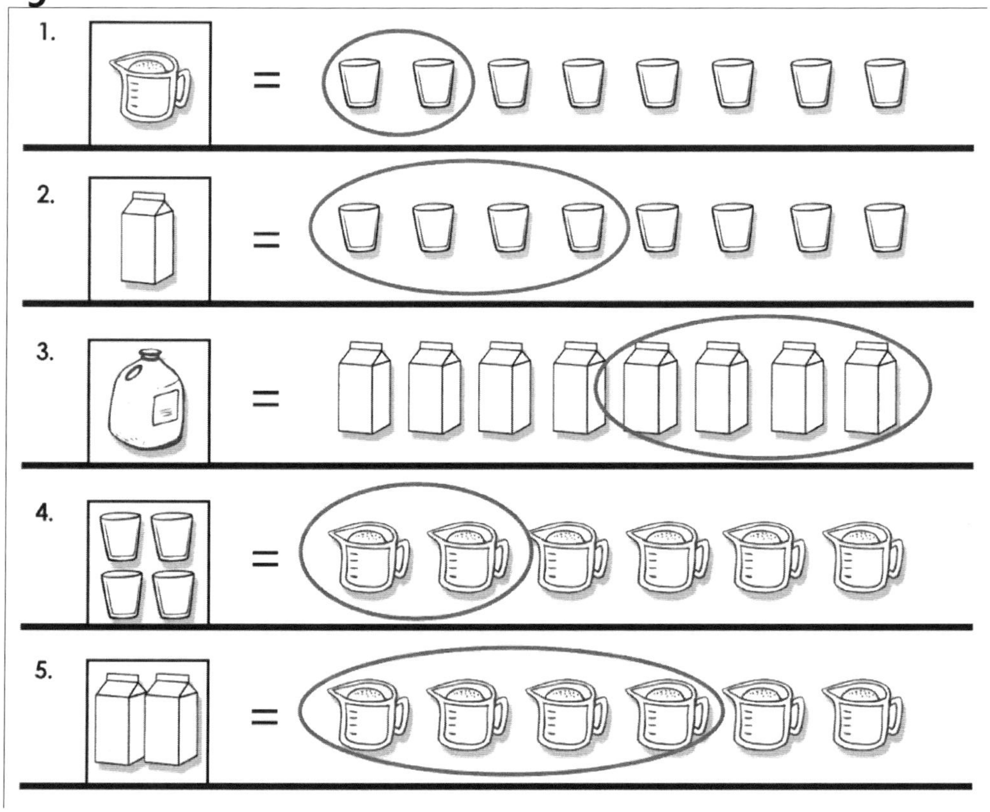


| Pg 109 | | | |
|---|---|---|---|
| **No.** | **Answer** | **No.** | **Answer** |
| 1 | 7 | 13 | 24 |
| 2 | 24 | 14 | 40 |
| 3 | 4 | 15 | 3 |
| 4 | 2 | 16 | 8 |
| 5 | 32 | 17 | 40 |
| 6 | 16 | 18 | 12 |
| 7 | 2 | 19 | 6 |
| 8 | 4 | 20 | 4 |
| 9 | 10 | 21 | 2 |
| 10 | 104 | 22 | 14 |
| 11 | 80 | 23 | 40 |
| 12 | 3 | 24 | 12 |

| Pg 110 | |
|---|---|
| **No.** | **Answer** |
| 1 | 20 gallons |
| 2 | 3 pints |
| 3 | 12 gallons |
| 4 | 16 ounces |

# *Chapter 8 - Fractions*

| Pg 112 | | Pg 113 | | Pg 114 | |
|---|---|---|---|---|---|
| **No.** | **Answer** | **No.** | **Answer** | **No.** | **Answer** |
| 1 | 1/3 | 1 | < | 1 | < |
| 2 | 2/3 | 2 | < | 2 | < |
| 3 | 1/4 | 3 | > | 3 | > |
| 4 | 2/4 | 4 | < | 4 | < |
| 5 | 3/8 | 5 | > | 5 | > |
| 6 | 4/8 | 6 | > | 6 | < |
| 7 | 3/16 | 7 | < | 7 | < |
| 8 | 9/16 | 8 | < | 8 | > |
| | | 9 | > | 9 | > |
| | | 10 | < | 10 | > |
| | | 11 | < | 11 | = |
| | | 12 | > | 12 | > |
| | | 13 | < | 13 | > |
| | | 14 | < | 14 | < |
| | | 15 | > | 15 | < |
| | | | | 16 | < |
| | | | | 17 | < |
| | | | | 18 | > |
| | | | | 19 | < |
| | | | | 20 | > |

| Pg 115 | |
|---|---|
| **No.** | **Answer** |
| 1 | $1\frac{1}{10}, 1\frac{6}{10}, 2\frac{1}{10}, 2\frac{3}{10}$ |
| 2 | $4\frac{4}{8}, 6\frac{2}{8}, 9\frac{3}{8}, 9\frac{6}{8}$ |
| 3 | $6\frac{1}{4}, 6\frac{2}{4}, 7\frac{1}{4}, 7\frac{3}{4}$ |
| 4 | $8\frac{1}{9}, 8\frac{2}{9}, 8\frac{3}{9}, 9\frac{1}{9}$ |
| 5 | $1\frac{1}{12}, 2\frac{3}{12}, 3\frac{1}{12}, 3\frac{8}{12}$ |
| 6 | $5\frac{1}{54}, 5\frac{2}{54}, 5\frac{3}{54}, 5\frac{7}{54}$ |

| Pg 116 | | Pg 117 | | Pg 118 | |
|---|---|---|---|---|---|
| No. | Answer | No. | Answer | No. | Answer |
| 1 | $\frac{4}{5}$ | 1 | $\frac{4}{5}$ | 1 | $\frac{4}{15}$ |
| 2 | $\frac{8}{10}$ | 2 | $\frac{27}{59}$ | 2 | $\frac{5}{9}$ |
| 3 | $\frac{5}{6}$ | 3 | $\frac{7}{7}$ | 3 | $\frac{5}{14}$ |
| 4 | $\frac{10}{12}$ | 4 | $\frac{9}{13}$ | 4 | $\frac{2}{8}$ |
| 5 | $\frac{8}{9}$ | 5 | $\frac{11}{15}$ | 5 | $\frac{9}{39}$ |
| 6 | $\frac{8}{14}$ | 6 | $\frac{70}{209}$ | 6 | $\frac{13}{39}$ |
| 7 | $\frac{5}{7}$ | 7 | $\frac{16}{22}$ | 7 | $\frac{7}{10}$ |
| 8 | $\frac{3}{4}$ | 8 | $\frac{21}{33}$ | 8 | $\frac{4}{15}$ |
| 9 | $\frac{5}{6}$ | 9 | $\frac{24}{45}$ | 9 | $\frac{10}{16}$ |
| 10 | $\frac{7}{8}$ | 10 | $\frac{104}{138}$ | 10 | $\frac{2}{7}$ |
| 11 | $\frac{9}{11}$ | 11 | $\frac{4}{6}$ | 11 | $\frac{2}{26}$ |
| 12 | $\frac{12}{15}$ | 12 | $\frac{7}{10}$ | 12 | $\frac{19}{62}$ |
| 13 | $\frac{12}{14}$ | | | 13 | $\frac{9}{24}$ |
| 14 | $\frac{2}{3}$ | | | 14 | $\frac{29}{54}$ |
| 15 | $\frac{6}{8}$ | | | 15 | $\frac{83}{98}$ |
| 16 | $\frac{4}{5}$ | | | | |
| 17 | $\frac{11}{13}$ | | | | |
| 18 | $\frac{7}{10}$ | | | | |

| Pg 119 | | Pg 120 | | Pg 121 | |
|---|---|---|---|---|---|
| **No.** | **Answer** | **No.** | **Answer** | **No.** | **Answer** |
| 1 | $\frac{14}{44}$ | 1 | $8\frac{5}{8}$ | 1 | $2\frac{2}{4}$ |
| 2 | $\frac{2}{10}$ | 2 | $3\frac{4}{5}$ | 2 | $5\frac{2}{6}$ |
| 3 | $\frac{11}{63}$ | 3 | $12\frac{7}{10}$ | 3 | $3\frac{1}{9}$ |
| 4 | $\frac{3}{90}$ | 4 | $4\frac{10}{15}$ | 4 | $1\frac{2}{13}$ |
| 5 | $\frac{6}{12}$ | 5 | $9\frac{14}{21}$ | 5 | $14\frac{10}{21}$ |
| 6 | $\frac{20}{30}$ | 6 | $13\frac{34}{42}$ | 6 | $10\frac{5}{30}$ |
| 7 | $\frac{3}{7}$ | 7 | $16\frac{8}{9}$ | 7 | $6\frac{8}{26}$ |
| 8 | $\frac{9}{24}$ | 8 | $23\frac{15}{29}$ | 8 | $7\frac{5}{17}$ |
| 9 | $\frac{14}{98}$ | | | | |
| 10 | $\frac{3}{10}$ | | | | |
| 11 | $\frac{2}{15}$ | | | | |
| 12 | $\frac{5}{12}$ | | | | |
| 13 | $\frac{1}{34}$ | | | | |
| 14 | $\frac{3}{8}$ | | | | |
| 15 | $\frac{7}{23}$ | | | | |

| Pg 122 | | Pg 123 | |
|---|---|---|---|
| No. | Answer | No. | Answer |
| 1 | $\frac{3}{3}, \frac{1}{3}$ | 1 | $\frac{9}{9}, \frac{1}{2}$ |
| 2 | $\frac{4}{4}, \frac{1}{3}$ | 2 | $\frac{2}{2}, \frac{3}{14}$ |
| 3 | $\frac{3}{3}, \frac{2}{5}$ | 3 | $\frac{3}{3}, \frac{5}{6}$ |
| 4 | $\frac{2}{2}, \frac{4}{5}$ | 4 | $\frac{4}{4}, \frac{3}{4}$ |
| 5 | $\frac{5}{5}, \frac{2}{5}$ | 5 | $\frac{18}{18}, \frac{1}{2}$ |
| 6 | $\frac{5}{5}, \frac{4}{5}$ | 6 | $\frac{3}{3}, \frac{8}{25}$ |
| | | 7 | $\frac{7}{7}, \frac{1}{7}$ |
| | | 8 | $\frac{27}{27}, \frac{1}{3}$ |

# *Practice Test Answers*

## Practice Test #1

## Answers and Explanations

**1. C:** Donald has five dollar bills, which totals \$5, and \$1.24 in change; the sum of \$5 and \$1.24 is \$6.24.

**2. C:** The diagram represents one whole, plus three-eighths of a second whole. Therefore, the diagram represents the fraction, $1\frac{3}{8}$.

**3. B:** The fraction, $\frac{2}{5}$, is equivalent to the fraction, $\frac{4}{10}$. The numerator and denominator of the given fraction are both multiplied by 2 to obtain the model for $\frac{4}{10}$; the fractions are proportional.

**4.2443:** To find their combined miles just add them together.

**5. B:** In order to find the number of cans of food he gave to the first charity, the number of cans of food he has left needs to be subtracted from the number of cans he collected; $1{,}082 - 602 = 480$.

**6. B:** The given model represents the fraction, $\frac{2}{9}$, which is approximately 0.22. The model for Choice B represents the fraction, $\frac{1}{8}$, which equals 0.125. This fraction is less than the given fraction. The fractions can also be compared by finding a least common denominator.

**7. A:** The sum of the two decimals is 10.80; the decimals are added just like whole numbers are, while aligning the decimal point.

**8. B:** If they lay the sticks end to end then you would just add the lengths together. First convert $\frac{7}{8}$ to $\frac{14}{16}$ then add that to $\frac{5}{16}$ to get $1\frac{3}{16}$.

**9. B:** The array represents the multiplication sentence, $4 \times 6 = 24$. Note. There are 4 rows and 6 x's in each row.

**10. D:** The model shows 35 counters, divided into 7 groups, with 5 counters in each group. Therefore, the model represents the number sentence, $35 \div 7 = 5$.

**11. B:** She runs $12 \times 8$ laps in all, or 96 laps.

**12. C:** Since he approved 13 trees out of every group of trees and surveyed 15 groups, he approved $13 \times 15$ trees, or 195 trees.

**13. 230**: In order to find the amount of money she can spend each day, 690 should be divided by 3; $690 \div 3 = 230$. Thus, she can spend 230 dollars per day.

**14. B:** The number of cupcakes sold can be rounded as follows: 80 cupcakes, 50 cupcakes, and 70 cupcakes, which sum to 200. Therefore, the best estimate for the number of cupcakes sold is 200 cupcakes.

**15. B:** The amount of money Lynn has to spend on groceries for the month can be rounded to \$300; $300 \div 4 = 75$. Thus, the best estimate for the amount of money he can spend per week is \$75.

**16. B:** The amount of money Carlisle charges per hair cut can be rounded to \$20; $20 \times 30 = 600$. Thus, his total charges are approximately \$600.

**17. B:** The missing number sentence in the fact family is the other division number sentence, which reads:$42 \div 6 = 7$.

**18. 477:** If he travels 572 miles and then 437 miles then he only has 477 miles left to go. 1486-572-437=477.

**19. 87 in.:** There are 12 inches in a foot. $12 \times 7 = 84$. Then divide 12 by 4 to get 3. 84+3=87.

**20. C:** As noted in the pattern, the product of 100 and 24 can be found by multiplying 24 by 1 and adding two zeros to the product. Thus, the product of 100 and 24 is 2400.

**21. 245.** Since she completes 35 each day, she has completed $35 \times 7$ situps after 7 days; $35 \times 7 = 245$.

**22. B:** The value of y is indeed 4 times the value of x. Note. 4 is 4 times the value of 1; 8 is 4 times the value of 2; 12 is 4 times the value of 3; and 16 is 4 times the value of 4.

**23. $93°$:** Since the angle of a straight line is known to be $180°$, then $38° \text{ } and \text{ } 49°$can be subtracted from that to get $93°$.

**24. D:** Multiply the 5 chicken coops times the 14 chickens to get 70. Then multiply the 6 barns times the 16 cows to get 96. Add those together to get 166.

**25. B:** A pentagon has 5 sides.

**26.** 4.22 > 4.2

.09 < .9

2.72 > 2.702

**27. D:** To multiply a whole number by a fraction, multiply the whole number by the numerator only to receive the product. When multiplying 16 by 1/5th, multiply 16 by 1, and leave the denominator as 5. The product is 16/5. Similarly, when multiplying 4 by 4/5, the product is 16/5.

**28. A:** The trapezoid is symmetric about the axis, thus showing at least one line of symmetry. The isosceles trapezoid does not have any more lines of symmetry. Therefore, it has one line of symmetry.

**29. D:** The number line is divided into fourths. Thus, between the whole numbers, 7 and 8, lie the fractions, $7\frac{1}{4}, 7\frac{2}{4}$, and $7\frac{3}{4}$. Point A represents the fraction, $7\frac{3}{4}$.

**30. B:** The number line is divided into tenths. Thus, between the whole numbers, 14 and 15, lie the fractions, $14\frac{1}{10}, 14\frac{2}{10} \ldots 14\frac{9}{10}$. The fraction, $14\frac{2}{10}$, lies two-tenths, or two intervals, to the right of 14.

**31. I,II,V,VI:** $7 \times 1 = 1, 7 \times 3 = 21, 7 \times 6 = 42, 7 \times 11 = 77$

**32. 281:** To find the difference just subtract. 3128-2847=281

**33. $11\frac{1}{4}$:** To find the length just subtract $3\frac{3}{8}$ from $14\frac{5}{8}$.

**34. I, III, VI:** $1 \times 42 = 42, 3 \times 14 = 42, 6 \times 7 = 42$

**35. D:** The measurements of the box can be rounded to 8 inches, 4 inches, and 2 inches. The volume of the box is equal to the product of the measurements of the length, width, and height of the box. Thus, the volume is approximately $8 \times 4 \times 2$, or 64 cubic inches.

**36. D:** If she needs to make 24 cupcakes and she knows the amount of sugar for 3 cupcakes then she just needs to multiply by 8. So $\frac{1}{4} \times 8 = \frac{8}{4} = 2$.

**37. C:** From 2:15 to 4:15, two hours have passed. From 4:15 to 4:30, 15 additional minutes have passed. Therefore, the elapsed time is 2 hours, 15 minutes.

**38. A:** There were 9 students who preferred Bushmaster Park; 9 students is more than any other number of students displayed on the bar graph.

**39. 36.** The possible meal combinations are equal to the product of the number of different types of each part of the meal. Thus, the possible meal combinations are equal to $3 \times 3 \times 2 \times 2$, or 36.

**40. D:** Five drivers drove at an average speed of 70 miles per hour, which is more than any other number of drivers, driving at a particular speed; three drivers drove at an average speed of 55 miles per hour, three drivers drove at an average speed of 60 miles per hour, and four drivers drove at an average speed of 65 miles per hour.

# Practice Test #2

# Answers and Explanations

**1. C:** The first room contains, $6 \times 9 = 54$, chairs. The second contains 32. $54 + 32 = 86$.

**2. D:** The amount of money she pays is equal to the sum of 3 dollar bills, or \$3, and 51 cents, or \$0.51. Thus, she paid \$3.51 for the sandwich.

**3. B:** The fraction, $\frac{8}{12}$, is equivalent to the fraction, $\frac{2}{3}$. The numerator and denominator of the given fraction are both divided by 4 to obtain the model for $\frac{2}{3}$; the fractions are proportional.

**4. B:** The first diagram represents 1 whole, while the second diagram represents $\frac{2}{5}$. Thus the diagram represents $1\frac{2}{5}$, in its entirety.

**5. B:** The fraction, $\frac{5}{15}$, is equivalent to the fraction, $\frac{1}{3}$. The numerator and denominator of the given fraction are both divided by 5 to obtain the model for $\frac{1}{3}$; the fractions are proportional.

**6. II, III:** $\frac{4}{6}$ and $\frac{6}{9}$ can both be reduced to $\frac{2}{3}$. This means they are equivalent.

**7. C:** The sum of the dollar amounts is equal to $\$156 + \$173 + \$219$, or \$548.

**8. B:** Since Andrea paid \$120 per month more last year, the amount she paid per month last year is equal to the difference of \$763 and \$120, or \$643.

**9. C:** The diagram represents the sum of $\frac{3}{10}$ and $\frac{8}{10}$, or $\frac{11}{10}$, which is equivalent to $1\frac{1}{10}$, or 1.10. The decimals, 0.30 + 0.80, can also be added, which equal 1.10.

**10. C:** The array includes 3 rows and 7 columns. Thus, the array represents the number sentence, $3 \times 7 = 21$.

**11. B:** Since Eli will equally share his crayons, he will divide 42 crayons into 6 groups; $42 \div 6 = 7$.

**12. C:** Alex will be $3 \times 12$ gallons of milk in 12 weeks, or 36 gallons of milk.

**13. C:** The number of candles sold can be rounded as follows: 20 candles, 40 candles, and 20 candles. Thus, a good estimate of the number of candles sold is $20 + 40 + 20$ candles, or 80 candles.

**14. B:** The distance Isabelle drives can be rounded to 1,500 miles; 1,500 miles divided by 5 days is equal to 300 miles driven per day.

**15. B:** The consultant's earnings can be rounded to $18,000; $18,000 divided over 6 months is equal to $3,000 per month.

**16. 640:** Each box contains 20 packets, so that's the same as $32 \times 20$, which is 640.

**17. 21:** If 1 pizza feeds 3 people then you can multiply 7 times 3 to figure out that 7 pizzas feeds 21 people.

**18. Part A: C:** The circle is divided into eighths and then 3 of them are shaded.

**Part B: D:** If you shaded 3 more of the eighths that would make $\frac{6}{8}$ which reduces to $\frac{3}{4}$.

**19. D:** Brad drives 275 miles each day. Thus, the total number of miles driven, over a period of days, can be found by adding 275 miles to the number of total miles driven for each previous day. In other words, after 4 days, he drove 1,100 miles. After 5 days, he drove 1,375 miles. After 6 days, he drove 1,650 miles. After 7 days, he drove 1,925 miles. After 8 days, he drove 2,200 miles.

**20. A:** The values in the second column are indeed 12 more than the values in the first column. Note. 16 is 12 more than 4; 19 is 12 more than 7; 24 is 12 more than 12; 26 is 12 more than 14; and 31 is 12 more than 19.

**21. C:** The total amount of money donated is $300 more each additional year. Thus, the total amount donated, over a period of years, can be found by adding 300 dollars to the amount donated for each previous year. In other words, after 6 years, the total amount donated was $1,750. After 7 years, the total amount donated was $2,050. After 8 years, the total amount donated was $2,350. After 9 years, the total amount donated was $2,650. After 10 years, the total amount donated was $2,950.

**22. D:** An obtuse angle has a measure greater than 90 degrees. It may be greater than 120 degrees, but that is not a requirement.

**23. 1930:** To find the answer multiply 386 times 5.

**24. A:** An acute angle is less than 90°. Answer A id the only angle less than 90°.

**25. A:** First add all of the fractions together to find out how much of the pie was eaten. $\frac{1}{4} + \frac{1}{8} + \frac{3}{8} = \frac{6}{8} = \frac{3}{4}$, so that leaves $\frac{1}{4}$ of the pie that was not eaten.

**26. Part A: B:** A triangle does not have any parallel sides.

**Part B: D:** Perpendicular lines always form a 90° angle. None of the sides of a hexagon form a 90° angle.

**27. C:** The number line is divided into tenths. Thus, between the whole numbers, 5 and 6, lie the decimals, 5.1, 5.2,5.3, 5.4, 5.5, 5.6, 5.7, 5.8, and 5.9. Point P represents the decimal, 5.8.

**28. C:** The number line is divided into fourths. Thus, between the whole numbers, 3 and 4, lie the fractions, $3\frac{1}{4}$, $3\frac{2}{4}$,and $3\frac{3}{4}$. Point C represents the fraction, $3\frac{3}{4}$.

**29. D:** To find the answer just multiply 14 times 22.

**30. Part A: 82:** To find the answer add up all of the numbers in the table. This gives the total number of students surveyed.

**Part B: B:** There are 10 5th graders that chose cats as their favorite. There are 30 5th graders total. $\frac{10}{30} = \frac{3}{10}$.

**31. C:** The 2 is in the thousands place. The 5 is in the hundreds place. The 7 is in the tens place, and the 3 is in the ones place.

**32. B:** 8 units make up the length and 5 units make up the width. Area is length times width, so $8 \times 5 = 40$.

**33. A:** There are 16 ounces in one pound. Thus, her approximate weight, in ounces, is equal to the product of 27 and 16; $27 \times 16 = 432$. She weighs approximately 432 ounces.

**34. 8.** There are 2 cups in 1 pint and 2 pints in 1 quart. There are 4 pints in 2 quarts. Thus, there are $4 \times 2$, or 8 cups, in 2 quarts.

**35. 96:** If she buys 6 packages of 12 then she buys, $6 \times 12 = 72$. She already had 24, so 72+24=96.

**36. 320:** If he uses 6 tanks then 1920 can just be divided by 6 to get 320.

**37. B:** The circle graph can be created by determining the fraction of students, with preferences for each season. The total number of students surveyed is 40. Thus,7 out of 40 students, or $\frac{7}{40}$ students, prefer Fall; 3 out of 40 students, or $\frac{3}{40}$ students, prefer Winter; 12 out of 40 students, or $\frac{12}{40}$ students, prefer Spring; and 18 out of 40 students, or $\frac{18}{40}$ students, prefer Summer. These fractions can be converted to the following percentages: approximately 18% prefer Fall, approximately 8% prefer Winter, 30% prefer Spring, and 45% prefer Summer. The circle graph, shown for Choice B, correctly represents these percentages.

**38. A:** There were 4 teachers who preferred Virginia; 4 teachers is less than any other number of teachers displayed on the bar graph.

**39. 24.** The possible outfit combinations are equal to the product of the number of different types of each clothing piece. Thus, the possible outfit combinations are equal to $2 \times 2 \times 3 \times 2$, or 24.

**40. C:** The score of 92 was received by 3 students, which is more than any other score received; 78 was received by 1 student; 90 was received by 1 student; and 79 was received by 2 students.

# *Online Resources*

Due to our efforts to try to keep this book to a manageable length, we've created a link that will give you access to all of your online resources:

**mometrix.com/resources719/ssnystg4mathwb**